CLING
FILM

"These poems are, apparently, for me because I laughed for an hour alongside Bethany Handley and, while I was laughing, I forgot about my pain."
– The Cyborg Jillian Weise

"These poems are mirrors, reflecting the ways society hasn't been designed with disability in mind... Bethany Handley's sharp observation and wit points out injustices but also transcends them... these poems aren't just for those of us who have experienced ableism and discrimination, but for anyone who values life."
– Joshua Jones

"A breathtakingly raw and beautiful collection of poetic snapshots that scream of authenticity throughout. *Cling Film* gives so much empathy and humanity in its pages making it not only a refreshing read but also a vital one, for a real depiction of the world."
– Connor Allen

"*Cling Film* holds up to the white light of the page the multi-layered micro-aggressions of ableism and asks us as individuals and as a society to do better. There is no looking away as Bethany Handley transforms the CCU into a forest filled with birds or herself into a transnational drug smuggler – be careful, these poems will change the way you see the world."
– Kim Moore

"At turns witty, surreal, razor-sharp, joyful, scathing, celebratory and unsparing, *Cling Film* brilliantly testifies to the mundane absurdities and ableist micro-aggressions of day-to-day life as a disabled person, at the same time as skilfully and subtly drawing the reader into its perspectives. Glorious, necessary reading."
– Polly Atkin

CLING FILM

BETHANY HANDLEY

SEREN

Seren is the book imprint of
Poetry Wales Press Ltd
Suite 6, 4 Derwen Road, Bridgend,
Wales, CF31 1LH

www.serenbooks.com
Follow us on social media @SerenBooks

ISBN: 978-1-78172-768-3

A CIP record for this title is available from the British Library.

The publisher acknowledges the financial assistance of the Books Council of Wales.

Cover artwork: Seren Books.

Printed in Bembo by 4Edge Ltd, Hockley.

Contents

Cling Film

Ableism. The act of wrapping the world in cling film.

ableism is the steel band around my wrist
with my name and a number for when you find me unconscious
you know to take me seriously

<del>Does she...?</del>

ableism is the government telling me to stay at home
so that if Covid takes my breath you won't have to watch

<del>Take a stand</del>

ableism is the interviewer who reassures
we don't see your disability

<del>Take a stand</del>

<del>Does she...?</del>

ableism is the chairless corridors
that command me to wait at home
quietly

<del>Take a stand</del>

or the dog shit you didn't pick up
that I am forced to wheel through
and it stains my wings

                                 or the absent ramps that stop me taking off
                   from the pavement and soaring up, up above Cardiff

                                                              ~~Take a stand~~

or the job that doesn't want
part timers

~~Take a stand~~

                                 or the surgeon's letters carved on my belly
                                                  that you can't read

or the train I can't take because I look
too healthy for that chair

                                              or the rusting car I'm not
                                                  allowed to drive

                                                              ~~Does she....?~~

or the *I'm sorrys*
scattered in rubber shavings

                                 ableism is the mate who said
                                 your illness doesn't bother me

                                      8

or the *you look well* on days
I hang my wings at home

Does she….?

or the glass on the tarmac that
erases my tread

Does she….?

or the activism that fights
for all

Take a stand

ableism is the face that asks
how do you dance?
but doesn't think to look up to the sky

Does she….?

or the film you've wrapped me in
as I move with palms open to the clouds
whilst yours are bound to the ground

Take a stand

ableism is the race you'll want me to run
one day to prove *how far I've come*

or the poems
you'll demand

                                        ableism is the cling film
                            you've wrapped around everything

                everything

I reach for your hand
but I can't feel your skin

                                        just the cling film
                                        that's hard to tear

pin a tail on the donkey

are you sure you can't feel your legs what about here
or here have you tried yoga black seed paste prayer
can't you even wiggle your toes do you eat gluten do
you believe in god veganism pilates hiding your pain
acupuncture paleo diets picturing yourself standing
do you take iron & b12
                too many supplements may cause paralysis
have you tried napping you're just young you'll grow out
of it have you tried counselling sea
                swimming increasing your salt
                        bog snorkelling
                                positivity
not being stressed do you keep a gratitude journal drink
        water electrolytes
                                climb trees with your eyes
have you tried loose leaf tea meditation
digital detox stroking a cat not letting on
                                        counting the stars
cutting out caffeine holding your breath
may i pray for you have you googled cures
do you get stoned manifest movement
do you crawl
                drag
                        hope
                                so your body remembers
                                        to move without wheels

can you get off the floor unaided   kneel on all fours
can you swim without sinking

whilst dragging your legs

have you tried cold water   warm water   putting your feet
in streams   doesn't the donkey require a tail

do you study photos of you hiking

watch how other people's legs move
                              so you don't forget

do you speak to your muscles

        move your legs with your hands
                              so they remember

have you tried hospitals in other countries

        getting pregnant

                        have you cast   spells
                                                in puddles

        do you even want   fixed
                                to be

The Heath

trees sipping the air

                    with the smokers

         entrance

                    wheeled into the darkness

                          date of birth?

                              name?

                     reason for visit?

        Bethany, what do you remember?

eyes becoming fossilised
chipping away at the rock to blink
room of limestone

              white

                dripping

                    no blue seats

                     just bodies

                              sitting   standing

beep

                  head on his lap

                s   l   e   e   p

     punctuated by names and groans

drawn down towards the floor

                discarded sick bowls on the windowsill

a soldier in combat gear
pushing an old woman in a wheelchair
whose battle?

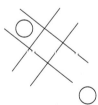

                                    Barbara Davies

an earthquake?
room trembling

smell of pine
    urine

the soiled minute
floating in the bleach

Claire Jones
I need a chair

a game of hangman

Claire Jones?
I need a chair

inflating
beep
blood pressure reading in waiting room

_ _ _ _ _ _ _ _ _ _ _ _

room slips anticlockwise
backs on floor   feet to sky
eyes slipped under facemasks

―――

a̶

Jakob Coleman

_ e _ _ _ _ _ _ _ _ _ _

another soldier

_ e _ _ _ i _ _ _ _ i _ _

Arthur Summers

_ e _ _ _ i _ o _ _ i _ _

I'm sorry, we're out of chairs

_ e _ _ _ i _ o _ u i _ _

B̶

we'll do it here if that's ok

_ e _ _ r i _ o _ u i _ _

beep beeep   beeeeepppppppppp

Đ

feet thudding

14

I'm the second hand
slipping off the clockface

Mum, you shouldn't have been discharged so soon

his hand on mine holding me in the room

_ e n _ _ r i _ o _ u i _ _

M̶

C̶

_ e n t r i _ o _ u i _ t

_ e n t r i _ o _ u i s t

Emily Crossland

Bethany Handley?

follow my finger

Bethany, what do you remember?

Arwyn Davies

s l e   e   p

look up for me

an open curtain

can you move your legs?

Someone else's blood
does your neck hurt?   stepped across the floor

push me away   ◯

pull me towards you

hello? we have a patient here with head trauma for a CT

the trees outside stretch to shadows
waiting at the door

Birdsong

There's an app that detects birdsong
        as you're walking through a forest

           translates trills into names and categorises
    this is the....
          hear how...
                  she came here from...
    ... and this is her story.

In the CCU I sleep in a forest
shielded by branches   and drip stands,
                wires

          and roots,

the red CPR button under my bed's
             a badger sett.

          Bay A's canopy song is sinking on the wind:

the steady sighs of 4a's drip
      3a's heartbeat beep launching
           from branches

        to the forest floor   in unsteady
                flight
                 the leaves
                    shaking
             as 5a sucks in oxygen

     2a groaning as she rolls
           onto her left side   in the pine needles
the sharp
     shrill emergency alarm of the
             little owl

      resus cart
         snapping twigs

silence following that can never
be silent

hesitant clocks marked
with day,
bright drawings of a sun   clouds

as unlike the forest,
the ward resists night

Bay A's voices
tethered together
like a network
of fungi
sending hope to sister trees

with one song.

Poems submitted by male doctors

1. Just get pregnant; it will help with the pain.

2. You're too young to be a wheelchair user.

3. You'll grow out of it.

A Swift's Flight

A swift, perhaps Earth's greatest aeronaut, calls her own name in flight.
The day her first wheelchair arrives she dreams she flies above Cardiff,
so sure in air she announces her motion as she soars,
following the streets like sand scattered through clasped fingers.

Rarely does a swift land on earth.
She rises up above the spitting salt of the sea and clouds,
she eats and sleeps and bathes on the wing, migrating across continents
until she is a glassblower in her own molten bubble orbiting the sun.

Grounded, a swift can't take off with ease;
each night she checks her soles for clues of what her skin should have felt.
Swifts' legs are fingers, not fists. They don't pound but stroke the earth.
She searches for cuts, grazes and bruises.

A swift wheels across the sky, flying to the moon and back
five times over in her lifetime.
Some days she forgets to wear shoes,
with narrow wings the colour of black locusts, spanning twice her length,
pooled blood turns her feet heather purple while resting on her perch.

limbs not walked on

And he informs me a leg is not a leg
if not walked upon; a leg not aiding
standing or walking is just a limb.

I see the air these paralysed limbs
displace, the atoms bouncing away
from skin, knocking against each other

like a Newton's cradle, limbs last named
hiking up the Nantlle Ridge, feet balanced
on the tooth of folded, tilted mudstone.

The limbs of Mynydd Mawr are resting.
The mountain is not waiting to unfold and march
but still it moves, each pebble slowly

slipping. A raindrop shifting silt. Each tree root
buries fingers further between the rock.
Each branch snagging the wind.

A leaf is still a leaf when not clutching a branch,
when a leaf curls and drops
to the ground, catching dew as if turning to metal.

Soon only the blade and veins of the leaf
remain: a moth held to the sun which welcomes
the light. When the river rises to snatch

the leaf's skeleton, swollen
and bruising with muddy run-off,
the water is more gelatinous than flowing
but the river is still a river.

if i could walk tomorrow
(if there was a miracle or something)

i'd hug my parents
                    standing hugs are sea rounded pebbles in the palm

my cat would have to learn to walk
                              no more lap rolling room to room

i'd go home
              up the six steps to my front door

i'd enter through the front door
                        and leave and enter again

i'd shower at home
                no more showers at leisure centres

i'd grab an iced oat milk coffee and sip it as
                                    i strolled around the block

i'd enter a building through the main entrance
                                with other people

i'd say hello, lovely weather to strangers
                              no dodging what's wrong with yous

i'd look up as i move
                  rather than down at the lifting tarmac, cracks and kerbs

i'd get off a train
              i wouldn't be left on a train

i'd see faces not crotches at meetings
                              no more counting chelsea boots and brogues

i'd visit friends, climb the steps to their doors
                                see them in their homes

no more strangers prodding my skin
                    enough of being a doctor's pin cushion

i'd say fuck you to the physio
                    enough of colour coded resistance and good efforts

i'd piss against a tree like a man
                    in hiking boots

i'd bury my feet in the sand
                    feeling sand grains and skin knocking against each other

i wouldn't dance
                    i pirouette faster on wheels than i ever could on toes

and no
                    i wouldn't run a fucking marathon

Not Your Counsellor

You tell me you've got bunions.
Tell me how it hurts to walk.
How you sprained your ankle
running that 10k you didn't train for.
You show me your paper cut. The splinter
sheltering under layers of skin.
Tell me how you've had that winter
cough for a few weeks now. You tell me
how you went to A & E for an ear infection.
How your period pain is crippling.
How smoking a joint left you calling
for an ambulance, thinking your heart
would rupture. You show me a photo
of your mother. Tell me she has MS.
Ask if I know that disabled boy you met
on the bus. You tell me about your partner's knee
replacement. How, for a few weeks he'll need a chair
like me. You tell me you've fainted once
so you get it. Went over the handlebars
of your bike as a kid and thought you'd broken
your neck. How you wore a neck brace
for a few hours. How you were paralysed
by fear. You know what I've gone through.
You get nosebleeds in the mornings. You see
my seated joy, my body of skin, bone, metal
and tyres, veer for me like a water diviner.

When I say I'm tired

Rest [rest] | the remaining part | the bee in the conservatory seeking
nectar from the houseplants | a settling | a wave hesitating on | the
beach | an interval of silence | the *oh I'm tired too* | from the writing
group | *juggling work and writing is so tiring* | I mean tired as in it took
my daily energy to transfer from my bed to my wheelchair | or drag my
paralysed legs up the twenty stairs to | bed | rest from old English *league*
or *mile* | the distance after which one resets | tired as leatherbacks
swimming for one hundred million years | it's a lie they rest retracted
into their shells | I'm not talking to non-disabled writers about fatigue
again | at rest | the fallen magnolia flowers I gathered as a kid and
placed in bowls of water on the table until they bled | away

Enough [*ih*-nuhf] | are you Disabled enough? | as in the man waiting
by the blue badge bay to say *this is a Disabled bay* | *they do check blue
badges here* | *is it valid?* | he sees my wheelchair with an | *oh* | puts his
window back up | sea grass ripped from the seabed by an anchor | the
Department for Work and Pension's fortnightly calls to ask how I've
achieved their | goal | *you sat up this week?* | *good* | *you have met your
work-related goal* | *you are on track for employment and may receive your* |
£292 for the month | *but you know you can work lying down?* | dahlias
blooming flames before | the frost came | my legs do not need fixing |
they are as ornamental as an | orchid's | petals

Adapt [uh-dapt] | a young house martin learning to leap into | flight
| a biological process of change by which an organism or species
becomes better suited | to its environment | ghost pipes growing in
dark forests who cannot reach | the sun | have no chlorophyll in their |
bodies | yet on they bloom | the adapted car I would wheel into and
drive to the top of Blorenge to breathe with the | mountain *oh* | *wait
you don't work or study 12.5 hours a week?* | *no* | *writing doesn't count as
work* | *you're not eligible* | *for a vehicle* | a butterfly fresh from its chrysalis
drying out its | wings

24

Attended work focused interview

Universal Credit is an in and out of work benefit. It has been introduced to give you the support you need to find and progress in work. We want you to be able to benefit from all the positives that work brings. During your weekly interview with our agent, we'll check what you've done to increase your chances of getting work or earning more.

-£1500

Monthly DWP Payment On Attendance of Interview

Can't you work lying down
with headphones on?
Your goal for finding work this month
is to learn to sit up.

Attended work focused interview.

+£292.11

I have a friend like you. Had.
Had a friend like you. He was
paralysed falling- fell flat
on his back he did. Six days later
he was dead. Wasn't the broken
back that killed him mind. It was
a blood clot. Just like that. Dead.
You might have read about it in
the newspaper? He couldn't
have lived in a wheelchair mind,
young active guy he was, but
sounds like you're doing
well.

Your work-related goal for this month
is to get used to your wheelchair.

Attended work focused interview.

+£292.11

There were people like you
on an ad I saw on my Mam's TV,
said we should approach you
cause you're lonely. Shouldn't
just stare. Do you approach people
in the shops? Don't you go out?
This month's goal: go and talk to strangers.
Aren't you brave enough?

Attended work focused interview.

+£66 (lose 55p for every £1 earnt)

I broke my leg. Couldn't weight
bear you see. Obviously nothing like
what happened to you. They gave me
a lift for the bath- you don't have
one of them? Bet you want to go
home, don't you? I was lucky, see,
I could hobble with my zimmer frame
to the bathroom. It's downstairs.
You don't have a downstairs loo?

Attended work focused interview.

+£69 (lose 55p for every £1 earnt)

People only think it's not much
if they've never worked. Never
known what it's like to earn.
I've always worked full time so
it would be a loss for me. You
worked full time, didn't you?
See you're used to spending.
If you've always claimed benefits
it's a lot of money. I have
single mums who've never worked –
it's a lot for them. They don't know
any different.

My body has many homes

the lady from the council asks if i'm homeless | i say my
body has many homes:

with the wave before it breaks | mist settling | above the water so there's
no sea or sky | just a space i float within | a movement then a settling |

with the tyre marks in the mud | splatters signing my wheelchair frame |
tread crunching acorn shells and brown leaves | like corn kernels between
teeth | spitting out the shells |

with the swallows retuning to the barn by the tree | i see when i close
my eyes | an oak with palms open to the sky | so old the hills cannot
remember a time before the tree |

on the footplate of my wheelchair | holding my feet above the earth |

i tell the lady from the council | i have a house | an ammonite of empty
twisting chambers | that i cannot return to | where my clothes and
unburnt candles live | where books wait with unbroken spines | that the
six steps to my door | are as steep and foreboding as a mountain peak
in a snowstorm |

a house | built over a slumbering coal mine | where even the ghosts have
left | the pit's darkness trapped | so it inhales its own exhalations

beneath my lino | the lady from the council knows | i'm staying in a
house | without doors | only windows and stairs |

home is somewhere you can enter | and leave and enter

the lady from the council asks if i'm | homeless |

Poem submitted by lady in red duffel coat at Lidl checkout

You're such an inspiration.
I'd rather die than be confined to a wheelchair.

I'm not advocating for all beauty spots to be tarmacked

The town is just the pattering of rain drops
on the storm drain, as the water runs

down the southern slope of Sugar Loaf's
carpark, seeking exits in the sandstone.

Bracken crackles louder than the cars below.
The uncounted blades of grass rush past,

competing in their daily chores.
The gorse is ablaze with hubris.

The leaves on the slumped trees are folding
and opening like fingers clenching and unfurling.

The fog. The fog clings to the hills like children
held afloat in the sea by their parents.

The paths up the hillside are trodden not carved,
feet have stamped away the heather and bilberries.

I sit in my van with the door open, the wind paws
at my skin, summoning me to follow the footfall

up the hips of the hill. My wheelchair, waiting
in the back, is not welcomed by scuffed paths.

I watch the raven wheeling in the hush
of the valley. I murmur to the wind

enough

I'm here.

Fare

I

I sit on the sticky backseat of his car. He leans in. Smiles.
Says *You've done this before*. Closes the door.

Slams the boot shut. Climbs into the front seat.
Looks back over his shoulder. *Just you today then?*

Graffitied shutters and drunk lights blink in the night.
A man sprints down the pavement. A cyclist cuts off the taxis.

II

At the club, I feel the queue's eyes heating my back,
branding a question mark between my shoulder blades.

The hand of the bouncer cups my thighs as he lifts me.
My arms around his neck, his sweat soaks my lower back

as he carries me up the stairs. His breathing heavier, landing
as condensation on the skin of my arms. I've never weighed more.

III

On the way home, I roll my spine into the seat, the leather cooling
my vertebrae one by one. He brakes. Red traffic light screaming. He leans

back towards me. *So what happened to you then?* He tells me
to *Think of five people. Three of them will have it worse.*

Have you tried prayer? He catches my eye in the mirror.
Who's meeting you at the other end?

I want to leap out at the traffic lights, slam the door,
but my freedom is locked in his boot.

That will be £14.

Shall you tell them, or should I?

A first date was going well – we both liked
theatre and the outdoors. I thought
the *Do you want children?* was keenness.

Not a *Can you have children?* His *I broke
my leg once and used a wheelchair   for a week*
was empathy, not silencing.

He asks *What happened?* politely, asks
Will you ever get better? with care. He says
he benches 80kg so can easily lift me.

He tells me my wheelchair is snazzy, asks how it folds.
Some days he tells me to leave my wheelchair
in the car. *I'll park close, you've got me.*

He invites me to his Friendmas. I shell
the sprouts, stir the gravy. After dinner, he sits
his mates down, turns to me. *Shall you tell them*

or should I? We don't have news. He doesn't have
commitment. His Christmas gift whispered in my ear
is *I've deleted Bumble* when we met on Hinge.

He tells the group I'm Disabled.
She's a wheelchair user.
But only sometimes.

Poem submitted by man in the gym

If celebrities on *Strictly* can learn to waltz in a few weeks, then you can learn to walk.

Don't you know walking is the secret to a long life?

Enough

The lady in the lane taps me on my   foot
but my foot feels   nothing.   I'm floating
on my back like a goose coming in to land too fast

while rolling upside down in the air to slow her flight.   The light
crackling through the water is a white net,   clutching
my skin like nerves sending signals   I can feel.

The lady tugs my ankle,   but my ankle and I aren't on speaking terms.
My legs are tied together at the knees to stop paralysed limbs   floating off
like sea otters clinging together so they don't separate   in their sleep.

The lady in the lane   says this space is only for disabled people
    I swim away, each arm reaching until she can reach
        no further, my legs bobbing behind me like goslings.

    I send waves   over the lane ropes as I turn   my head
      side to side   to gasp for breath.
        At the wall, I place my palms flat   on the side

      push my weight through   my shoulders
    reclaim my skin and bone   from the body of water
lifting myself into my watchful wheelchair.

The lady from the lane approaches me
on poolside to apologise. She informs me
she's chair of the disability group

and I am disabled   enough.

Poem in which I'm a transnational drug smuggler

The guy in front of me is told to remove his leg. He unscrews
it and places it in the tub with his luggage. We watch
his leg disappear through the rubber curtain

as he hops through the airport scanner. His stump
is swabbed alongside another guy's empty boot,
a tube of toothpaste and a wallet. I'm asked to wheel

past the metal detector and to park myself
where the other travellers await their bags.
A female guard cups my arms, my waist, my breasts.

She asks me to raise myself above the cushion, squeezing
her hand into the gap between my skin and chair.
Below, my five-hundred-pound pressure cushion

protects my skin, bags of coke stashed where the gel
should hold my form. Each bum cheek is perfectly imprinted
in bleached powder. Later, when the taxi driver asks

whether my wheelchair is to support
my benefits claim, I'll smirk and nod.

You cannot slice warm bread

She'll trawl through charity shops for shed skins, emerge
with elasticated waistbands she can tug over atrophied legs.
Red and fierce she'll roll onto the high street, all sharp edges
and 110 psi. She'll pick out pinpoint stilettos, gold glittery,
still in their box. Too impractical to wear to that wedding,
the kind that do not give to your foot. She'll wear them to Lidl.

Every door will become a millimetre wider as she passes through,
splinters bouncing off her push rims. Each muscle spasm
will be a thunderclap. At the theatre, her paralysed leg will kick
the head in front. She will tell the woman it's the wind
or perhaps the ghost of the woman who wore these shoes before.

The ends of her hair will be snappable, so caked in mud where they rest
on her wheels whilst her shoes shine like streetlights on their footplate.
She'll plant sweet peas in her wellies, their stems more ambitious
with each cut. Some days she'll think she's weak when pushing
against cracked tarmac but her tyres will just lack air. She'll place neon
pink straws on her spokes so her body is not a shadow. She'll do pull ups
from her chair, gold shoes suspended in flight, lifting her joy like a dumbbell.

Her grief will fade to the hum of a damp finger tracing the rim of a glass.
Entering the beer garden, a glass of pinot resting between her thighs,
a man will hold the door open but will not step back. She'll leave
her tread across his white trainers like a slap. People will ask
if she's a student or here for work experience.
She'll smile, say this is not her first life.

Hiya Butt Bay

Castors to the sky, face to the sea,
I'm sitting on my back wheels, leaning against my friend
on Rest Bay beach as we sink into the wet sand.

Her weight wills us closer to the waves, driving us
forwards like she's back in a scrum, gripping my handles,
her feet digging as I clasp my push rims.

We wheel over a sandcastle, sink into its moat.
The turret's flag flies from my spokes,
crushed walls in my tread. Dog walkers and families

stare as we giggle, my wheels
submerged to the axle. A man approaches us,
clears his throat, informs my friend that when he takes

his mother-in-law out, he finds
it's best to drag her backwards. I give him
my *piss off mate, we're doing fine thanks* look.

We try it anyway, slowly turning
our backs to the sea,
admire our tyre marks stretching their limbs.

We see the children pretending to be a train
as they jog down our tracks and we're pushing
quicker towards the water, sand surrendering.

I used to chase footprints that obscured
my own, moved within another's trace.
Now I survey my trenches with delight

(you could read them from a drone)

you wouldn't guess they're footprints:
two unsteady lines claiming the land.

Acknowledgements and Thanks

Thanks to the editors of *Country Living, Poetry Wales*, Nine Arches Press, and *Barddas* where some of these poems first appeared. 'Pin a tail on a donkey' was longlisted for the 2023 National Poetry Competition.

This chapbook explores a snapshot of time in my life where I was new to ableist intrusions. Thank you to my gorgeous family and friends for bringing so much joy, love and resilience.

Thank you to my brilliant agent Amandeep Singh for your invaluable advice and support and to my editors Rhian Edwards and Zoë Brigley, and the rest of the team at Seren, for your expertise and wisdom.

Bob Walton, thank you for your unwavering belief in my work and for giving me the confidence to share my poetry. You've been such a compassionate friend and mentor and without you this chapbook wouldn't exist. Megan Angharad Hunter, thank you for your infectious love of writing and for your unconditional support and thoughtfulness. Ailbhe Darcy, thank you for inspiring me to pursue poetry and activism. Kim Moore and Owen Sheers, thank you for your generous mentoring.

Diolch o galon to the staff at Literature Wales for nurturing me as a new writer and poet. You have gifted me the means, the confidence and the community to write. Time spent at Tŷ Newydd, the National Writing Centre of Wales, enabled me to have an accessible space, free from the barriers of my every day, to write and to discuss ideas.

The Society of Authors' Contingency Fund also supported me in writing this chapbook, for which I am very grateful.

Diolch yn fawr iawn to the Disabled community for showing me life can be just as beautiful on wheels.